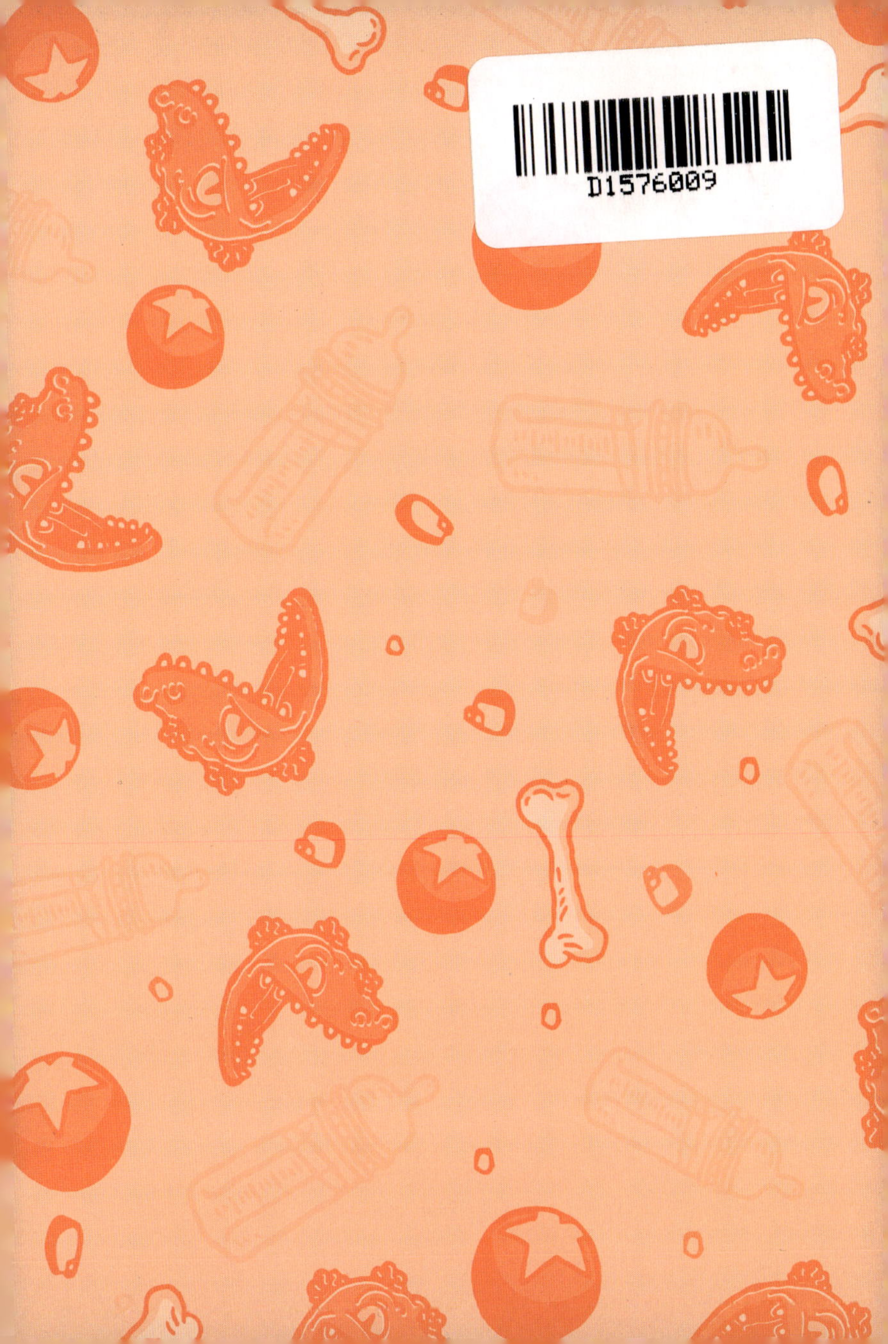

nickelodeon™

Rugrats™

Guide to
Adulting

Written by
Rachel Bozek

Contents

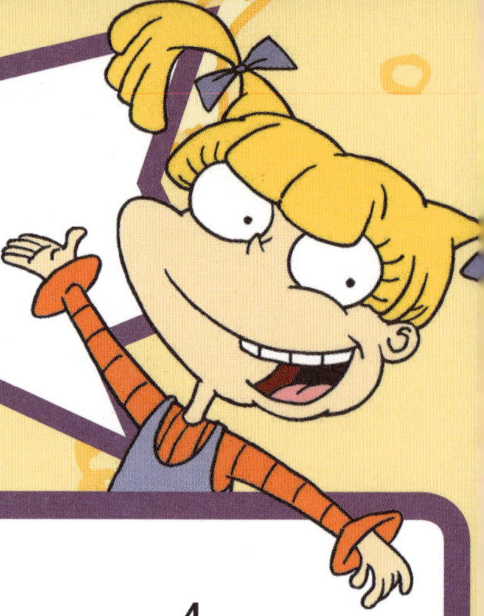

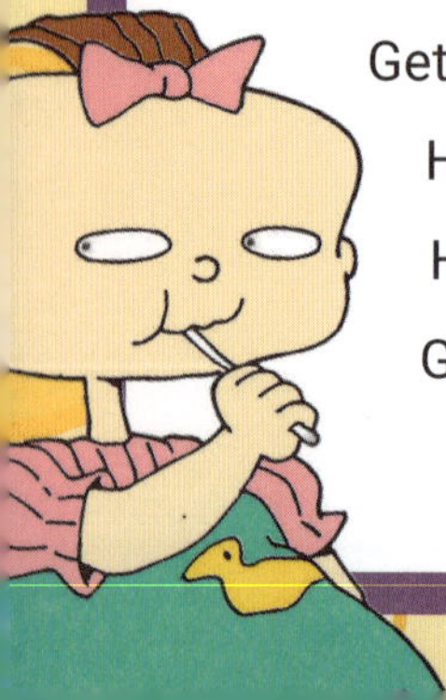

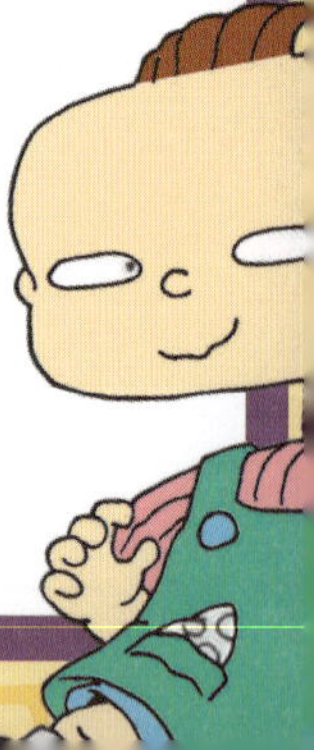

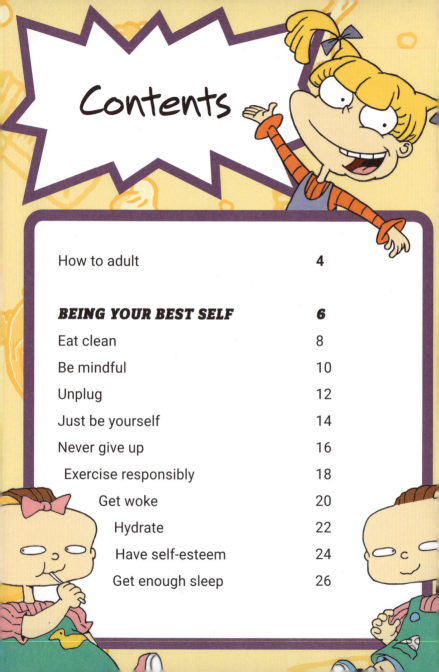

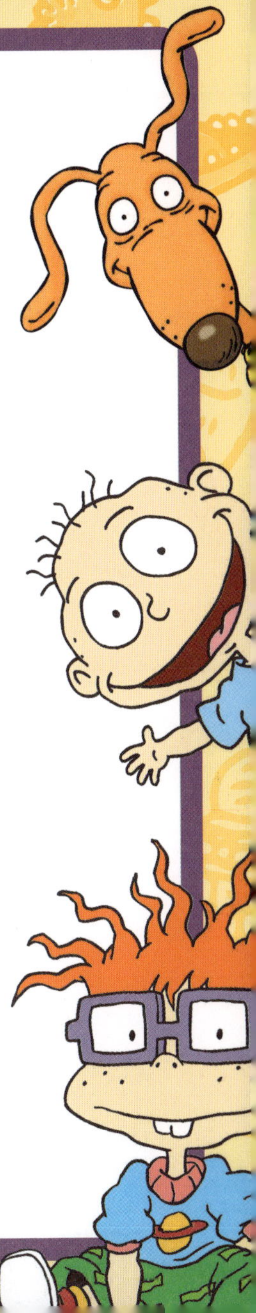

How to adult

Congratulations, you're a grown-up!
You've busted out of the playpen, traded
diapers for a potty, and kicked the binky habit.
Even though you might be unemployed or
sharing an apartment with seven of your
closest childhood friends, you can vote,
drive a car, and stay up past 7:30. Winning.

But adulting is scary as heck.
You have 'sponsibilities that
require more than a "cup
of jobe" to tackle. And
without mom and dad
to cushion your falls,
you need to learn the
art of self-care.

Luckily, Tommy,
Angelica, Chuckie, and
the Rugrats can help
you become your best self.

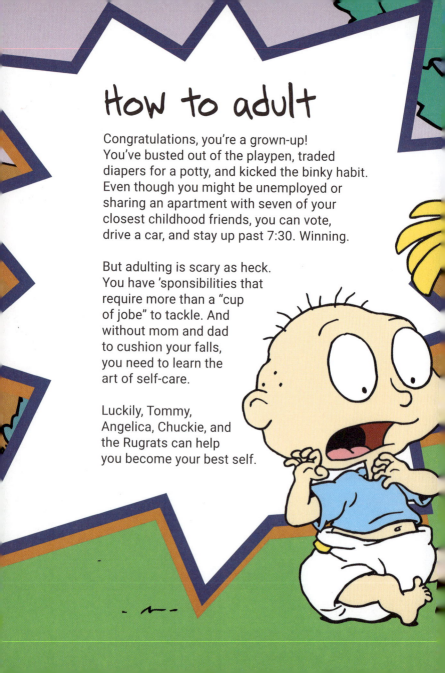

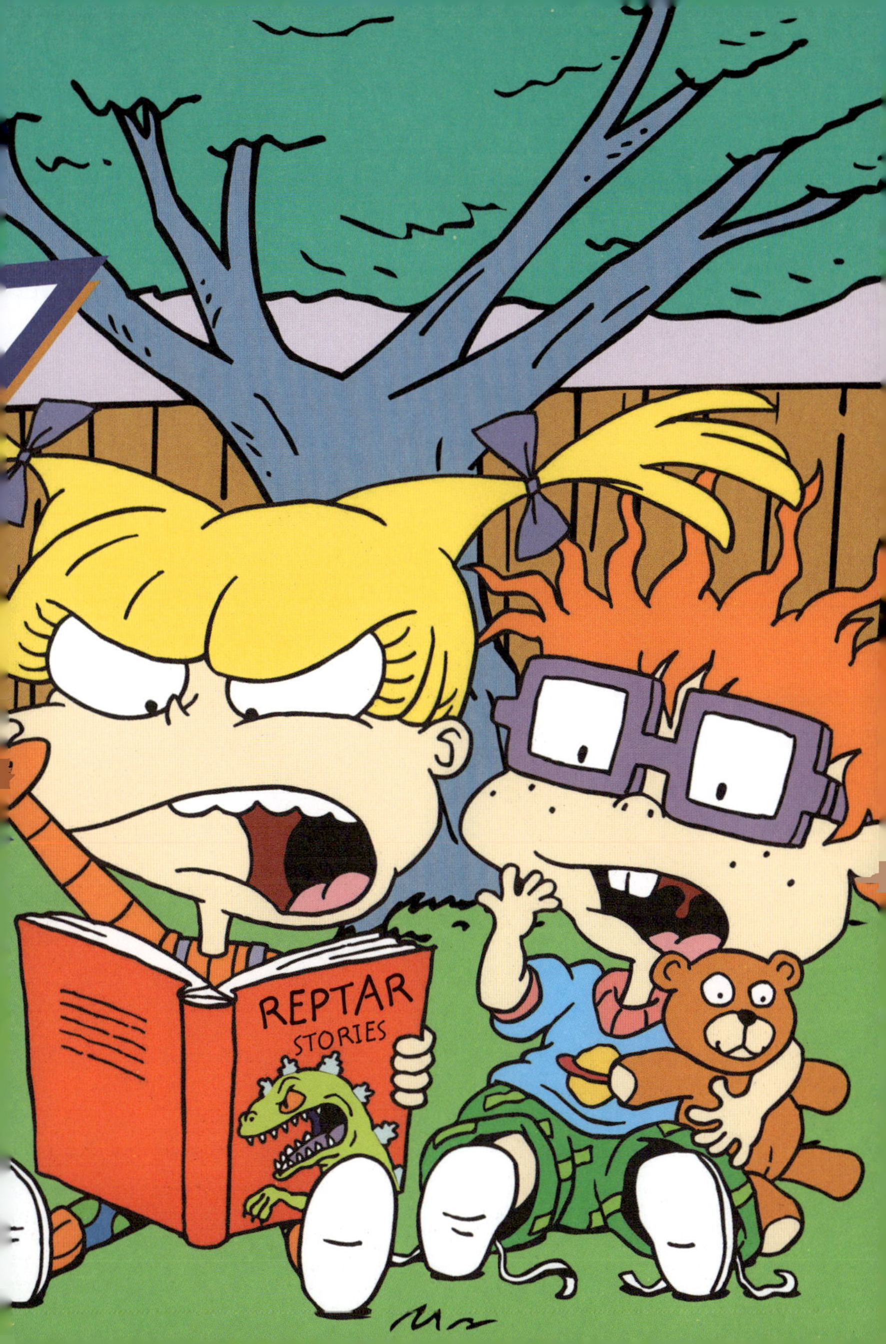
REPTAR
STORIES

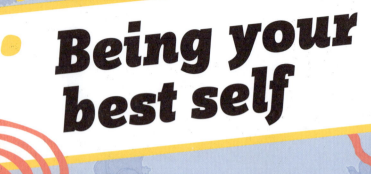

Being your best self

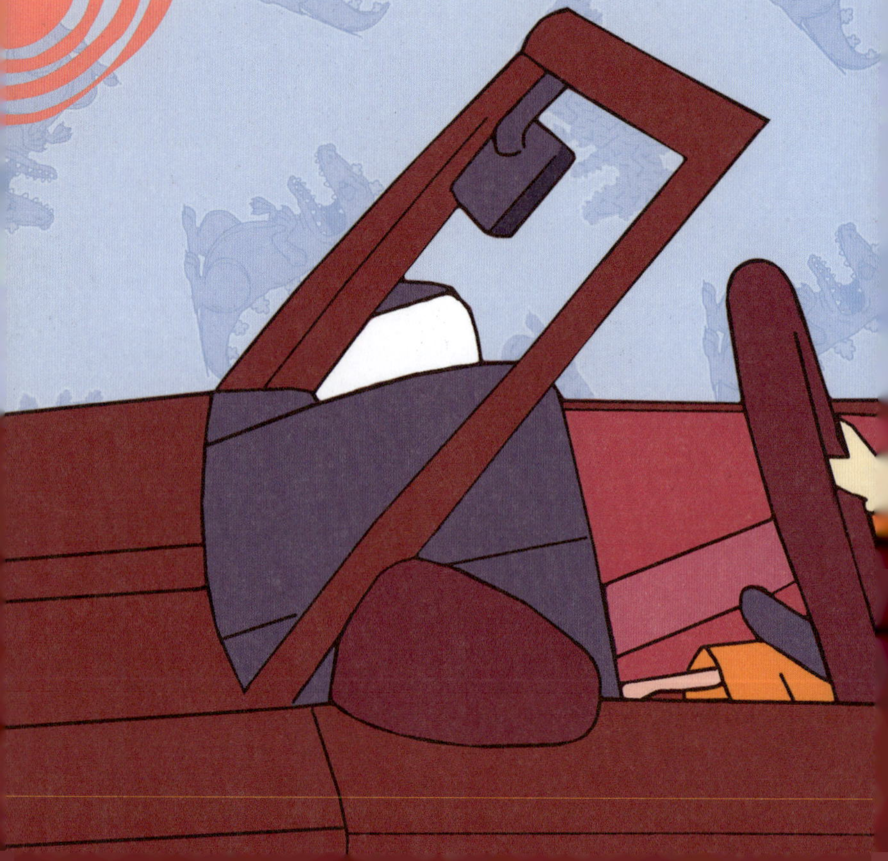

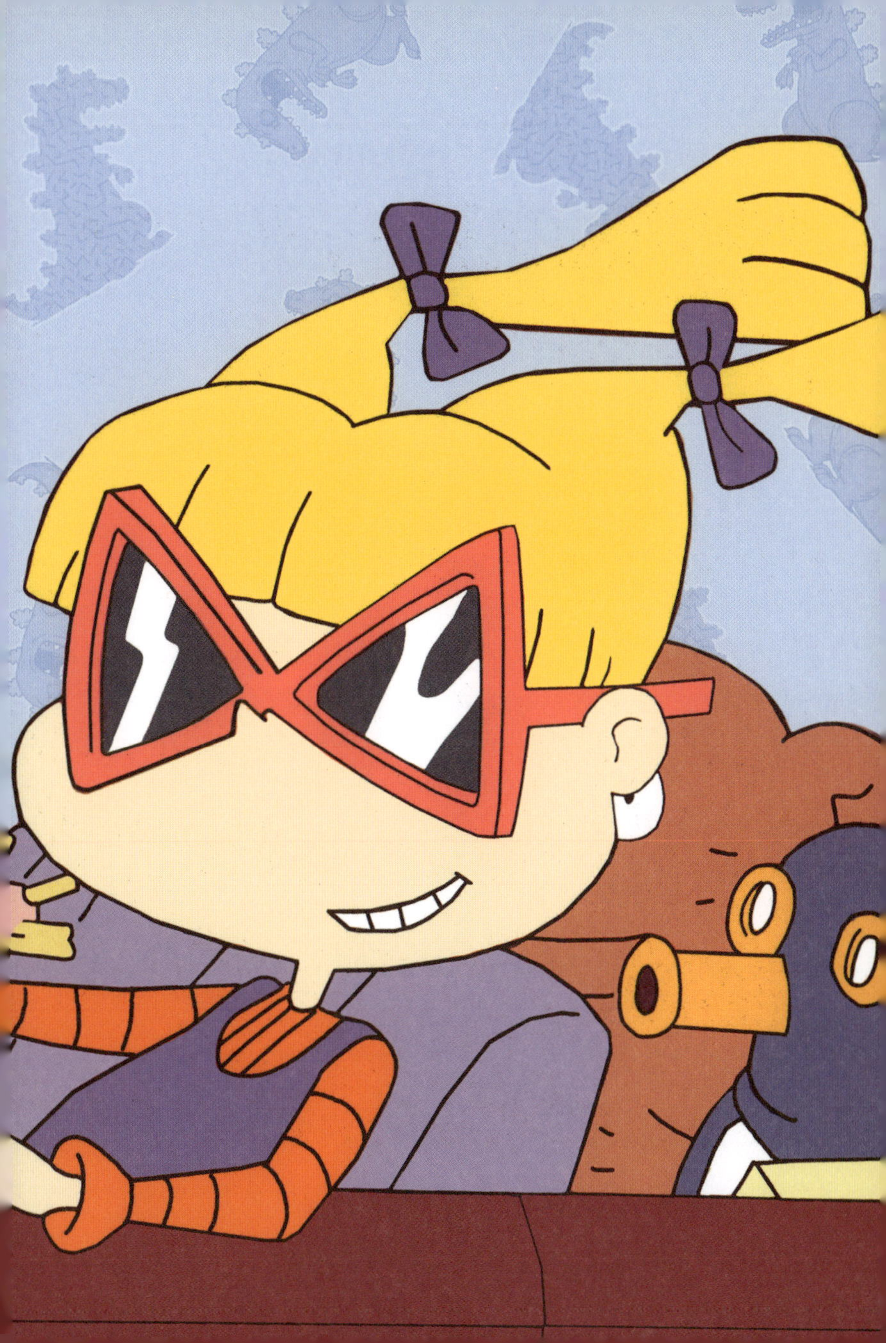

Tommy: "Are you sure it's okay to eat this?"
Phil: "It's all natural!"

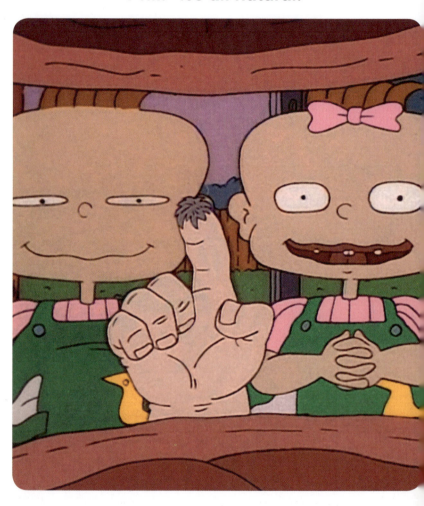

Tommy Pickles and Phil DeVille: "Psycho Angelica," Season 4, Episode 5 (August 1997)

Eat clean

Trans fats. Sweeteners. Heck, your bottle of juice could be full of squished GMO apples! Even Tommy knows that natural foods don't always go down easily, but the right diet will keep you healthy enough to conquer the highest slide on the playground.

#BetterThanKale #PaleoPickles #RawFood

Be mindful

Be present in the moment, even when you're surrounded by garbage. Literally. Just follow these simple steps:

1. Take a deep breath.
2. Forget about everything else that's going on around you.
3. Say, "Namaste right here and chill."

#LifeIsGood   #Mindfulness   #NoBadVibes

"Ah! Nothing like a nice, soft pile of garbage."

Chuckie Finster: "Mr. Clean," Season 3, Episode 20 (March 1994)

"The TV was our best friend. It was our window to the world. The source of all our joy. And now it's gone."

Chuckie Finster: "Kid TV," Season 3, Episode 23 (May 1994)

Unplug

Does the WiFi failing terrify you more than that time your mom forgot to pick you up from preschool? Embrace chances to put down the phone, turn off the TV, and recharge. Just be sure to search "how to live off the grid" before you banish your devices.

#DisconnectToReconnect #DigitalDetox #ICantEven

Just be yourself

Babies don't care what anyone thinks about their onesie, the way their dad styles their pigtails, or the brand of diaper they're wearing. Channel Tommy Pickles and be bold. Ignore body-shamers and enjoy just being the person beneath the cute, super-itchy outfit your mom made you wear.

#Mood   #NakeyIsNakey   #BeYou

"Nakey is good! Nakey is free!
Nakey is nakey!"

Tommy Pickles: "Naked Tommy," Season 3, Episode 15 (January 1994)

"No, Ice Cream Mountain is real! I just know it is. It just *has* to be!"

Angelica Pickles: "Ice Cream Mountain," Season 2, Episode 5 (October 1992)

Never give up

Maybe you're buried in student debt, living in your childhood bedroom, or can't land a job a high schooler could have. Go ahead and throw that temper tantrum. But be sure to pick yourself up off the floor and wipe away those tears—you have some mountains to conquer!

#ShePersisted #ClimbEveryMountain #LifeGoals

Exercise responsibly

Sure, you want to be fit, but if you're training for a mud run, smashing three HIIT classes a week, and sweating it out in hot yoga before brunch on Sundays, you'll soon burn out. Angelica knows the importance of recovery time. You don't want to end up with a cramp on leg day, bro.

#FitnessJourney #BabiesWhoLift #FitOver4

"Don't you babies know anything? You gots to wait an hour after you eat before you can tie shoes. It's a rule."

Angelica Pickles: "Tie My Shoes," Season 6, Episode 15 (April 1999)

"You know, my mom wears pants and she's a girl."

Phil DeVille: "Clan of the Duck," Season 4, Episode 10 (October 1997)

Get woke

Who says boys can't wear girls' clothes?
(I see you, Lil DeVille.) Take inspiration
from Phil and Chuckie and trade your shorts
for skirts if you want to. Social awareness
starts in the playpen, so crawl away from
those gender-specific toys and stay woke.

#WCW   #BettyWearsThePants   #YasssQueen

Hydrate

Juice is delish and milk does the body good, but you know the importance of drinking water for your health. Much like Al-Sabu, not even scorching-hot asphalt can keep you apart from your reusable bottle of organic, maple, protein, or just plain old tap water.

#PremiumWater   #ZeroWaste   #HydrateOrDie

"It's more important than cookies!"

Al-Sabu: "Heat Wave," Season 4, Episode 7 (September 1997)

"If Angelica is ever going to make it in a male-dominated power structure, she's got to eat, breathe, drink, and sweat self-esteem."

Charlotte Pickles: *"Princess Angelica,"* Season 3, Episode 14 (December 1993)

Have self-esteem

Angelica knows her worth—and so does her mom. But your parents can't always be there to remind you how awesome you are. Clap back at snowflake-haters, trolls, and anyone else who thinks you're less than. If someone's still throwing shade, take their cookies.

#ReclaimSnowflake   #ThisBabyCan   #NoTrolls

Get enough sleep

It's no secret that getting a full eight hours of sleep on the regular is key to staying healthy. When you're feeling tired, it's okay to crawl into bed, tuck yourself in tight, and put your phone on silent. You'll wake up with all the energy you need to scale a jungle gym—or face the morning commute.

#SleepEasy #CribLife #SelfCare

"I'm heading home to have myself a juice, snuggle with my blankie, and go nap-nap."

Tommy Pickles: "Showdown at Teeter-Totter Gulch," Season 2, Episode 4 (September 1992)

Winning at work

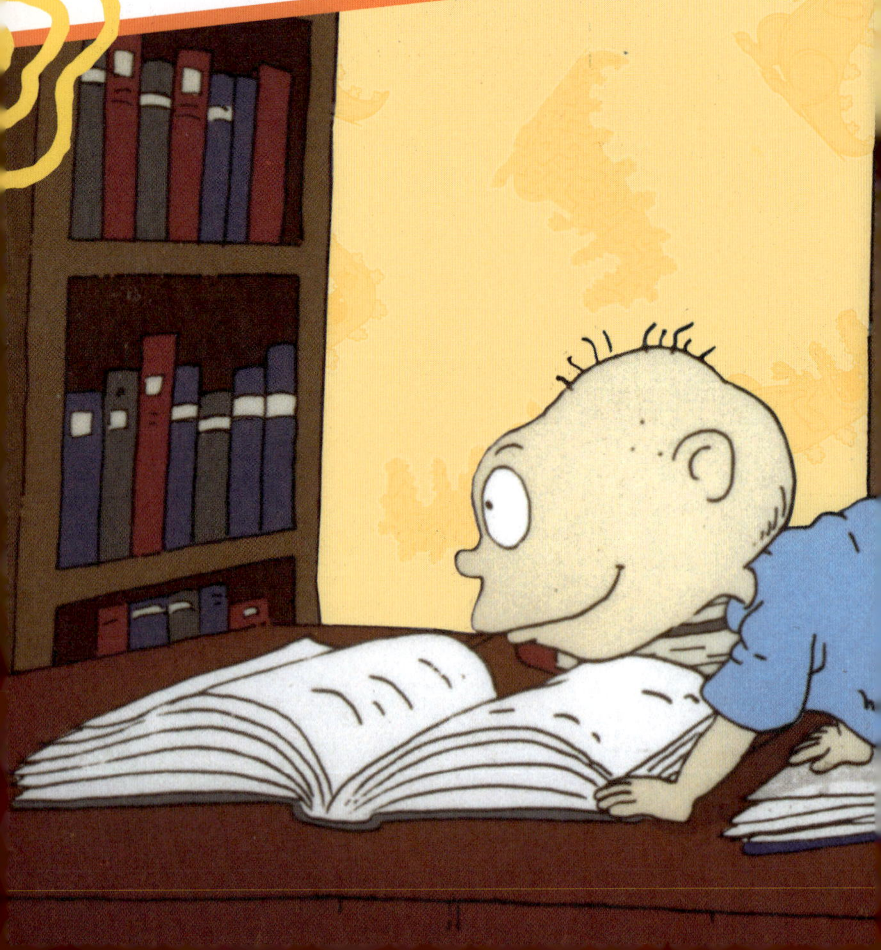

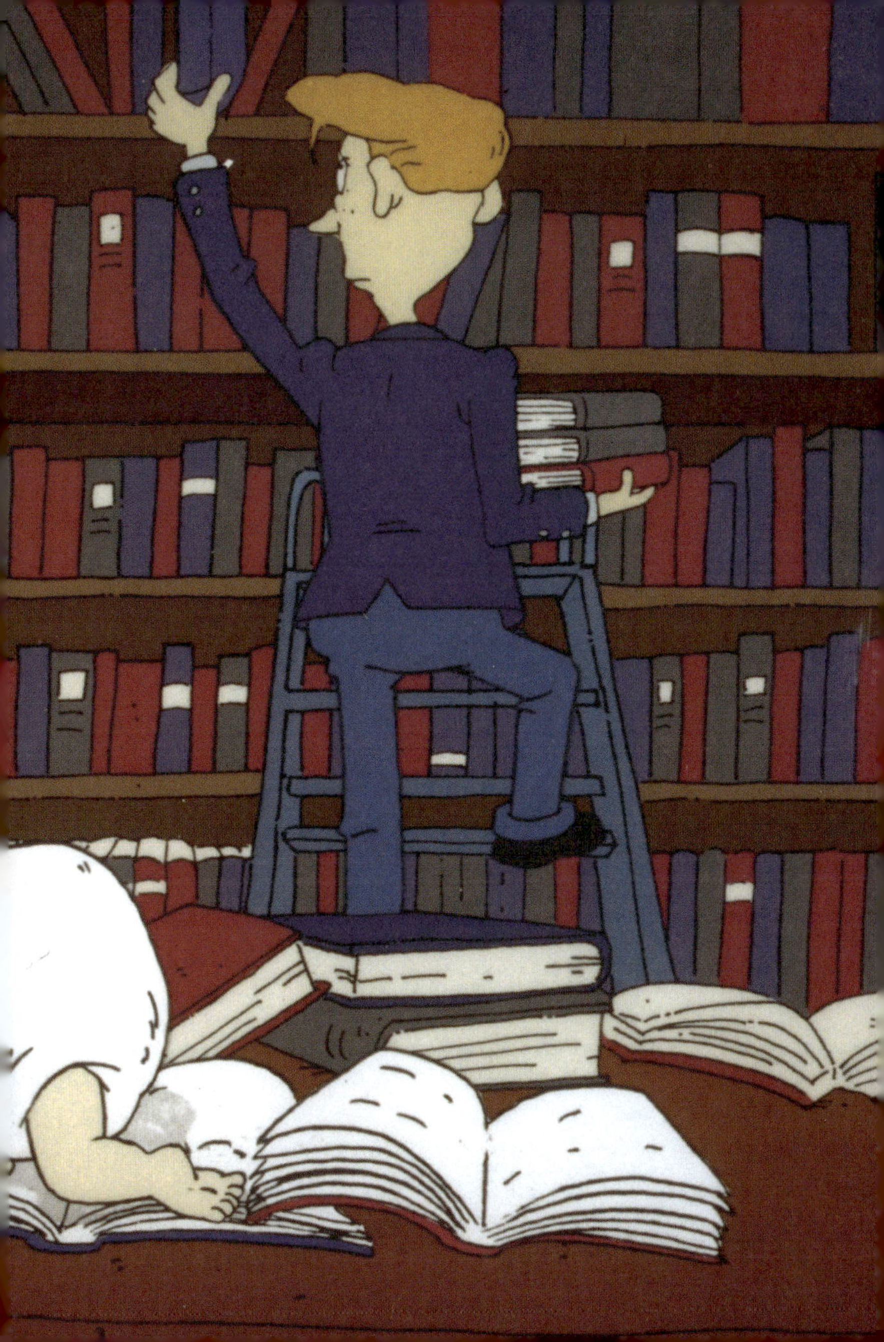

"I have 'sponsibilities now . . . That means I'm not allowed to have fun anymore for the rest of my life."

Angelica Pickles: "Angelica's Birthday," Season 3, Episode 13 (December 1993)

Be responsible

Sure, being a grown-up has its perks, but adulting also means dull duties: having a job, paying rent, and caring for an office plant that miraculously resurrects itself when it's finally watered. On her third birthday, the cold, hard realities of getting older hit Angelica harder than a napless afternoon.

#Preach   #AdultingIsHard   #ThisIs3

Think for yourself

If you're like Chuckie and constantly second guessing yourself at work, stop using someone's picture-perfect social media account as your life coach and do your own thing. You'll soon be bossing it—and any tyrannical toddlers that may come along.

#YouDoYou #ChuckieTakeTheWheel #BossIt

Angelica: "Do you always do everything I say? If I told you to jump off a bridge, would you?"
Chuckie: "Probably."

Angelica Pickles and Chuckie Finster: "Driving Miss Angelica," Season 2, Episode 25 (May 1993)

"The world is my toaster!"

Chuckie Finster: "Under Chuckie's Bed," Season 3, Episode 16 (January 1994)

Stay positive

Maybe you're facing monsters under the bed or trying to complete job applications on a cracked phone screen. Whatever the challenge, try to see the world through rose-gold-tinted glasses. You'll sleep better in your big-kid bed when you do.

#Blessed #AttitudeGoals #DontBeAscared

Balance work and life

Getting the balance right between work and life ITRW isn't easy. Yeah, you want to have a corner office by the time you're 35, but you also don't want to miss out on a box-set binge with bae. If you feel like your life is a hot mess, back away from the computer—or the chocolate pudding—and reassess.

#FOMO #FirstWorldProblems #DontMakeMeAdult

Didi: "It's 4 o'clock in the morning. Why on earth are you making chocolate pudding?"
Stu: " 'Cause I've lost control of my life."

Didi and Stu Pickles: "Angelica Breaks a Leg," Season 3, Episode 7 (November 1993)

"I don't have that much time, Angelica. I have to take my afternoon nap."

Chuckie Finster: "The 'Lympics," Season 4, Episode 6 (September 1997)

Manage your day

You don't need a lifestyle app or a bullet journal to master your work day. Just follow Chuckie's pro tips.

1. Sort out your priorities. (Naptime, obvi.)
2. Make time for you. If you need the potty, go.
3. Don't let the group chat distract you from your schedule. There will be time to catch up with your work BFF at lunch.

#NaptimeIsNonNegotiable #ToddlerPriorities

Negotiate

When the ball in your personal playground gets chucked over the fence, take a deep breath and strategize. How can you get what you want? Keep it high-key like Tommy and make yourself heard. After all, a baby's gotta do what a baby's gotta do!

#WorkIt #KeepYourEyeOnTheBall #CryBabyCry

"Why'd you stop crying? You coulda got anything you wanted!"

Phil DeVille: "Barbeque Story," Season 1, Episode 2 (August 1991)

"Angelica, we've been playing lemonade for a very long time now. I was just thinking: you're gonna share those dimes with us, right?"

Tommy Pickles: "Angelica's Last Stand," Season 4, Episode 10 (October 1997)

Ask for a raise

Sometimes life—or Angelica—gives you lemons instead of your fair share of cash. If you feel like you've been burning the midnight (lemon) oil at your desk, be like Tommy and ask your boss to fill up your piggy bank. Who knows—you might even get quarters instead of dimes.

#YouDeserveIt #WhenLifeGivesYouLemons

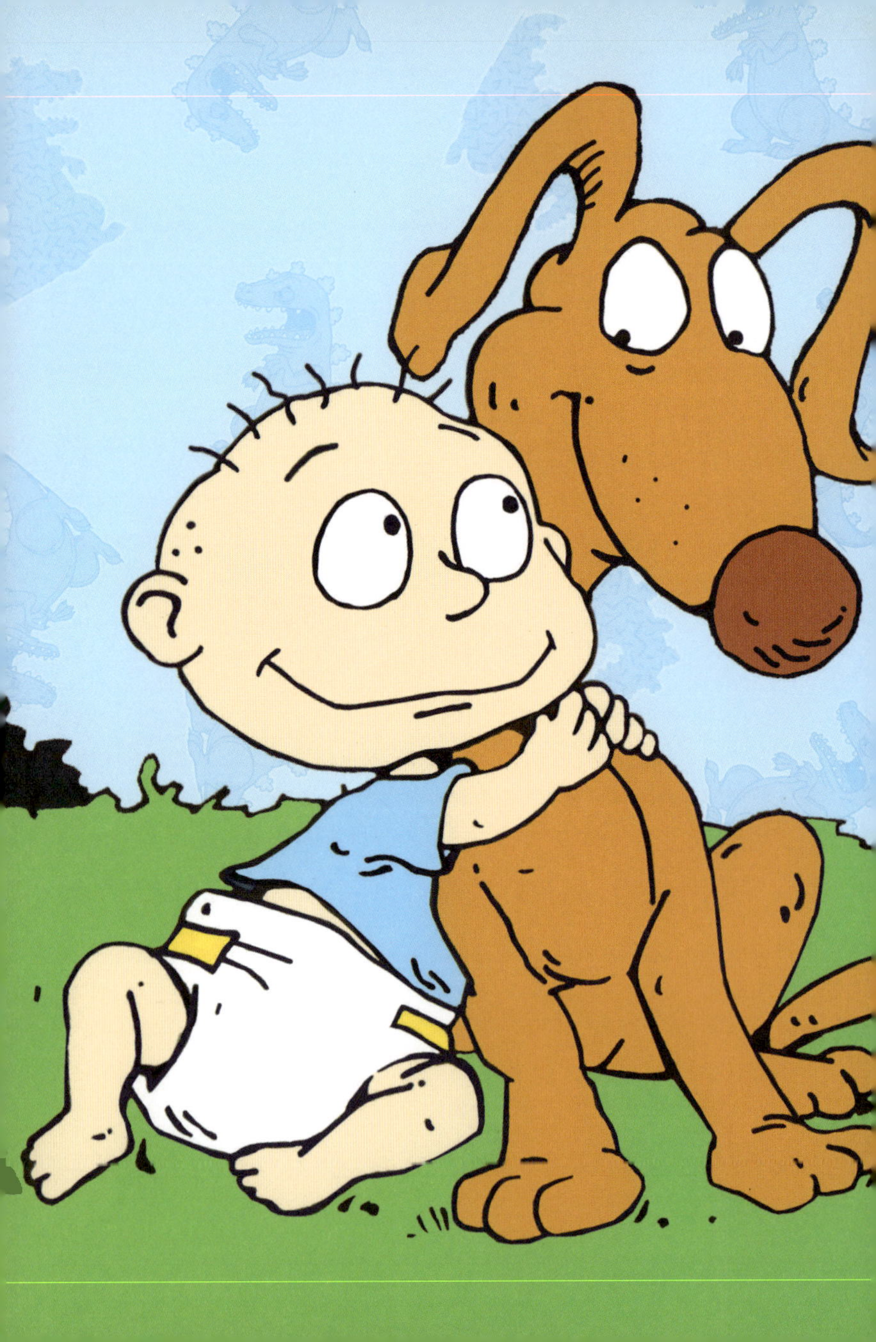

Nailing relationships

Be kind
to others

Take Charlotte's advice and play nice with your friends—ulterior motive or not. If you have no chill, you're going to be burned when no one wants to share a portion of fries with you, or follow you on social media. So let someone borrow your Cynthia doll, even if you really don't want them to.

#StayInYourLane #ShareTheLove

"Angel, when you don't share, well, it . . . it won't look good on the application for Harvard."

Charlotte Pickles: "Educating Angelica," *Season 4, Episode 9 (September 1997)*

> **"I might push you off your bike, or crash into it, or maybe even throw it out a window. But I'd *never* steal it!"**

Angelica Pickles: "The Tricycle Thief," Season 3, Episode 3 (October 1993)

Be honest

Real talk: Angelica might not be the nicest kid on the block, but at least she's legit. If somebody calls you out for being a bougie baby or a salty toddler, own it. It's better to be true to yourself than to pretend to be something you aren't. That's just fake news.

#LiveYourTruth #KeepIt100 #ThisIsMe

Be good to your fam

Your bro might spit up on you, your dad is more interested in his inventions, and Grandpa doesn't understand a word you say. But these are your people. Nobody's perfect, but blood is thicker than an avocado-kale smoothie, so tell them how much you appreciate them.

#LoveYourTribe #FamGoals #ILYSM

"Even when you gots a stinky diapee, you're still the little brother that I prefer."

Tommy Pickles: "Music," Season 6, Episode 13 (March 1999)

Chuckie: "You saved my life."
Tommy: "It was worth it, Chuckie. Even if all my blood comes out and I shrivel up . . . ."

Chuckie Finster and Tommy Pickles: "The First Cut," Season 5, Episode 7 (August 1998)

Love your best friend

If you're like Tommy, your biggest fear isn't a papercut, identity theft, or posting a makeup-free selfie—it's losing your best friend. You'll put yourself in danger to protect your bestie no matter what, and you know they'd do the same for you.

#BFFs   #BestFriendGoals   #AllTheFeels

Love others

Loving your family, your squad, and your boo takes effort, but of course you're willing to do anything for them. If agreeing to be part of a human-wave machine so your cousin's doll can waterski isn't relationship goals, what is?

#AnythingForThem #HighKeyLove

"I never knowed loving somebody was so much work!"

Chuckie Finster: "In the Naval," Season 4, Episode 12 (October 1997)

"This playground is for good kids who get along and play nice."

Tommy Pickles: "Showdown at Teeter-Totter Gulch," Season 2, Episode 4 (September 1992)

Stand up to bullies

TFW you get an ice pop shoved down your diaper and it's not even naptime . . . Bullies are the actual worst, but Tommy knows how to deal:

STEP 1: Stick up for your squad.
STEP 2: Tell the bully to stay in their lane.
STEP 3: Kick back with a bottle of juice.

#Respeck   #ByeBullyBye   #ZeroTolerance

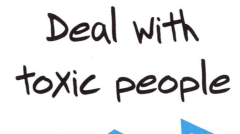

Deal with toxic people

When someone cray is ruining your day, your life, or just a game of Chutes and Ladders, don't just stand by. Follow Susie's lead and tell the Angelicas of the world to chill out or get out. Nobody needs those negative vibes.

#GoodVibesOnly #ToxicToddlers

"I am rubber and you are glue. Whatever you say bounces off of me and sticks to you."

Susie Carmichael: "Susie vs. Angelica," Season 2, Episode 25 (May 1993)

"I felt like a toy without batteries. But that's love sometimes."

Angelica Pickles: "Angelica's in Love," Season 2, Episode 5 (October 1992)

Survive a breakup

Whether bae is too attached to mommy to commit or you both decide it's time to hop on your trikes and move on, breaking up is rough. Take Angelica's advice:

1. Blast those feel-good Cynthia tracks.
2. Comfort eat Reptar Bars.
3. Resume normal tantrum-throwing and baby-terrorizing activities.

#SorryNotSorry   #LoveFail   #OnToTheNext

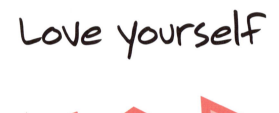

Love yourself

If you don't care about you, then no one else truly can either. Angelica may be extra sometimes, but she knows her self-worth, and she isn't afraid to remind anyone who forgets. Remember—those dumb babies are lucky to have you in their lives.

#MyOwnBestFriend #LoveYoSelf #Slay

"Sometimes I wish I could be you, just so I could be friends with me."

Angelica Pickles: "The Family Tree Part I," Season 5, Episode 12 (September 1998)

Senior Editor Tori Kosara
Editor Beth Davies
US Editor Kayla Dugger
Designers Sam Bartlett and Rhys Thomas
Design Assistant James McKeag
Pre-Production Producer Siu Yin Chan
Producer Louise Daly
Managing Editor Paula Regan
Managing Art Editor Jo Connor
Art Director Lisa Lanzarini
Publisher Julie Ferris
Publishing Director Simon Beecroft

Dorling Kindersley would also like to thank Alexandra Maurer, James Salerno, and the wonderful team at Nickelodeon; Steve Crozier, Chris Gould, and Anna Pond for design assistance, and Allison Singer for editorial help.

First American Edition, 2018
Published in the United States by DK Publishing
345 Hudson Street, New York, New York 10014

Page design copyright © 2018 Dorling Kindersley Limited
DK, a Division of Penguin Random House LLC

18 19 20 21 22 10 9 8 7 6 5 4 3 2 1

001–313291–Oct/2018

Published in Great Britain by Dorling Kindersley Limited.

A catalog record for this book is available from the Library of Congress.

ISBN 978-1-4654-7550-3

DK books are available at special discounts when purchased in bulk for sales promotions, premiums, fund-raising, or educational use. For details, contact: DK Publishing Special Markets, 345 Hudson Street, New York, New York 10014 SpecialSales@dk.com

Printed and bound in China

A WORLD OF IDEAS:
SEE ALL THERE IS TO KNOW

www.dk.com
www.nick.com

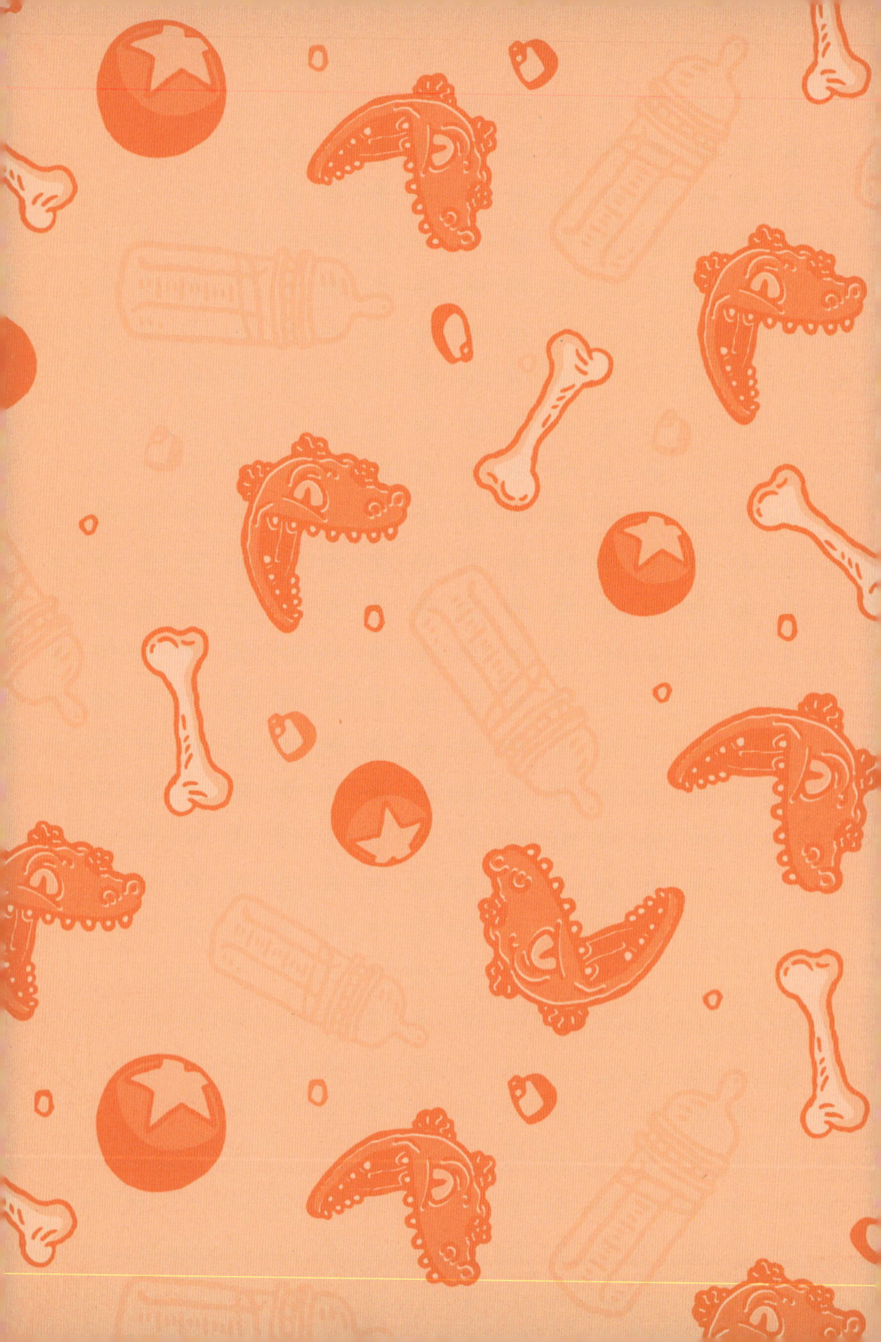